"Niki Tulk's exquisite *O* begins and ends with the numerical zero, the null, the void, the mouth that opens for 'the primitive word at the threshold of speech.' In the infinite *O* we find a fable of cross-species mothering. We find Ophelia in the non/sense of her song. We find another 'o,' a little o, raped and betrayed by the law. In myth, poem, found-text, fragment, and a final interview about the unsolvable problem of writing trauma, Tulk ingeniously spins a hypercube of desire, rage, sorrow, and most of all love as she opens to the unavoidable anguish and necessary power of mothering daughters in and against the perpetual violence of the patriarchy otherwise known as our lives."

—Julie Carr, author of *Sarah—of Fragments and Lines*

"The deeper I waded into Niki Tulk's *O*, the more I awoke. These poems throb in the shadow of poets like Anne Sexton, Muriel Rukeyser, and take up the challenge of philosopher Hélène Cixous, whose feminist writings urged women to 'write her self.' As Whitman responded to Emerson's call for the great American poet, so Tulk answers Cixous' vision—and oh girl, does Tulk succeed. These poems grow from personal and literary history and breathe themselves into being on the page. They 'crashjangle' us through the veil of patriarchy which, as Tulk writes, gendered violence is part of the fabric. Tulk is an interdisciplinary artist who sees the world and language with clarity and vision and delivers a song we have all been hearing in our heads but have never until this point been able to name. *O* is an ambitious, imaginative, mind-bending, heart-breaking, and world-creating collection that establishes Tulk as an original voice in feminist literature. I cannot wait to see what she does next."

—Michelle Bonczek Evory, author of *The Ghosts of Lost Animals*

"Niki Tulk's *O* is a devastating, multi-layered book of poetry that reconstructs relationships between language and the landscapes of gendered violence. Her exquisite poetic sequence knits together an operatic range of vocal registers, from fable to incident report, from performance score to how bodies keep score, to dream evocations haunted by Ophelia's rivers and the white talons of owls. This unique and necessary work heals bone deep by 'making real,' in ways that must be, and are here, reimagined."

—Lee Ann Brown, founder of *Tender Buttons Press*

"With rhythms and nods to Shakespeare and the tradition of storytelling and fable—and yet entirely alive and contemporary, entirely her own—Niki Tulk's *O* is a book that readers will consume breathlessly in one sitting, and then again and again. This is an urgent book, capturing what it means to experience, withstand, and witness sexual violence, and how survivors must rebuild their worlds and reinvent the language to do so. Tulk's *O* does just that work; it is a beautiful book about our darkest human experiences."

—Lynn Melnick, author of *Refusenik*

"In *O*, Niki Tulk offers readers a rare poetic gift: complex, interlocking and linguistically gorgeous slivers of story—both formally inventive and emotionally transparent—which gradually cohere into a portrait of heartbreak. A girl trades her feet for feathers, but barely takes flight. A daughter is harmed, and her mother marches forth for justice, unmet. In piece after piece, Tulk tells us everything we need to know, but strive not to. She pours the dangers of quotidian life into mythic forms that throw larger-than-life shadows, and suddenly we see, we believe. This book is magic."

—Heather Harpham, author of
Happiness: The Crooked Little-Road to Semi-Ever After

NIKI TULK

INDEPENDENTLY PUBLISHED BY
DRIFTWOOD PRESS

Independently published by Driftwood Press
in the United States of America.

Managing Poetry Editor & Interviewer: Jerrod Schwarz
Poetry Editor: Andrew Hemmert
Images: Hermann August Cappelen,
Robert Havell Jr., & John James Audubon
Cover Design: Sally Franckowiak, Jerrod Schwarz,
& James McNulty
Interior Design: James McNulty
Copyeditor: James McNulty & Jerrod Schwarz
Fonts: Merriweather, Pirata One & Trajan Sans Pro

First published July 26th, 2022
ISBN-13: 978-1-949065-21-3

Please visit our website at www.driftwoodpress.com
or email us at editor@driftwoodpress.net.

Contents

THE MANY FACES OF O
From "Shakespeare's Nothing" by David Wilbern

Nothing nil null nome naught nought: mathematical terms

zero and cipher share the same arabic root: sifr

sifr: secret letter or code, empty

void vacancy absence lack

negative nothing (threat) / positive nothing (creation)

hole/whole

circle/cycle/orb/ring/wheel

a matrix: stars, planets, orbits, celestial

womb, testicles, semen, eggs, eyes

womb/genitals/ mouth/eyes/egg

medieval topos of the enclosed, circular garden: virgin's womb

tomb/pit/hell

(tomb is the womb's reciprocal)

the devouring maternal mouth

God/heavenly spheres

a cosmos of concentric spheres

necromantic circle: summon spirits

research is all circles

a primitive word at the threshold of speech

an infinity of nothings is nothing, and also infinity

1

A Fable:
Part I

A weary traveler came to an inn and, on finding it full, climbed up a tree. Before long a bird came to her and promised her the whole sky for breakfast if she would only exchange her human feet for the bird's wings. It was a business transaction, pure and simple. The woman pondered, and as she pondered she noticed the tree felt strong, the leaves felt like fur, the traveler had never felt so safe the world beneath like a river. She said yes. The bird left, a storm came and enveloped her. The traveler fell into a deep sleep. The next evening she awoke and the air was calm. Her arms were feathered; resting beneath her pelvis, two claws.

The wind lifted the owl's body. To the vastness, she sang. The sky beat at her, azurite and cold.

It was near the end of twilight, tree and bird drenched with dark. Her feathers thin, more a membrane, eyes turmeric gold as with all owl eyes, whirring in the gathering gloam. Watch for the scuttle of tiny feet, the prickle of mouse, the scramble of mole. The owl and thin carving of moon, hiss of nearby sea.

A baker loved a bird and it was this way. The baker stirred and kneaded the grain soft on skin, a half-shade lighter than sand. Waiting for the bread to rise, the baker wandered the tideline, foam stirring at his feet, the sharpness of claw and beak, the gathering steam on windows on mouths.

Her talons gripped his arm and the softest thing in the world were her feathers, no longer membrane, but plump with longing. The baker whispered recipes, add this and then this and a loaf will rise so firm and full and brown and ripe with field fruit and then we can eat together, my love, we can eat together.

The wedding date was chosen, the moon itself was mantilla. Time is feathers in topsoil surrounded by roots. In the night wind the barley heads shiver, a field's wedding song.

The birth was at the new moon, no midwife the under-growth wet with blood. The girl had two mouths and ten feathers. The feathers were hope and bone and dissent, tremor on her shoulders. The owl mother left for a time, to wash herself in the sea. From the waves, she heard the mouths of her daughter, singing.

2
Big O

"There is a willow grows aslant a brook,
That shows his hoar leaves in the glassy stream.
There with fantastic garlands did she come
Of crowflowers, nettles, daisies, and long purples,
That liberal shepherds give a grosser name,
But our cold maids do dead men's fingers call them."

– Gertrude
(Hamlet, Act 4, Scene 7)

O is a daughter. O has a daughter. O is a mother without
a daughter. O had a daughter. O was a daughter and lost her
mother. O waits in a womb. O wants a womb to wait in. O
wants her daughter. O had a mother.
O's mother is trying to find her:
have you seen a girl dressed in dead men's fingers?

When you went to gather
flowers it was the wrong
season everyone said so
and had been saying so
ever since well before
the skull was
a beach, the frozen
letter a line of geese
tracking skywards away
from winter, but
you went anyway;
the leather on your feet
scraping the cliff
leaving no marks, no
scar.

There are no pansies in Denmark.

You clenched fish scales, brine, a stone
soaked dark with sea-tide, pressed
red clover
Denmark's national flower
to the Queen's skin, your brother's hand
Trillium pretense. Red clover
contains estrogen-like compounds.
You gave them estrogen. In handfuls.
(Just because? or in case? in spite?)

But more, purple northern marsh orchid
Dactylorhiza purpurella
Sprouting in dune slacks
where wild strawberries grow. Maybe

you crushed some in your hand, fingers
sweet now, red, plucked at nothing
                                    nothing.

You did not forget *Taraxacum*
asperatilobum. Dandelion.
Greek: *taraxos (abnormal health condition)*
          akos (remedy)
          taraxo (I have caused)
          achos (pain)

I have caused you pain (say it)
Pain and remedy; pain and no remedy
As a mild bitter vegetable (both root and leaf)
dandelion stimulates the tongue's
discernment
for bitter tastes.

And not rosemary. Blackberry: *Rubus hobroensis.*
In labor *Rubus hobroensis* will increase the activity of uterine
contractions when they are feeble
it has been found serviceable in after-pains.

The fruit is, sweet.
(pressed black eyes sprout from thorns)
Taste it
you sing:
And of all Christian souls, I pray God. God b' wi' you.

After this the play says: *Exit.*

                    In only this, you follow the script.

O knows that the sheets are clean only
when you beat them on rocks. She
watches the women
flay laundry by the river.

The women sing as they work:

Bury him bury him low in the ground
where the worms will eat his hands
and his fingernails will stop growing:
excavation is not a crime
crime is not excavation.

Who laid him in the cold earth?
Will they also lay her?

O thinks of their questions.
Their questions think her.
How many times (here is O's question)
can you tell one story and each time
that story gets whiter until there is no stain?
there is no stain no proof no evidence.

In her mind O crushes
cloth against stone:
again, again, again.

Her name: O.

O: the shape an eye makes when dreams are wet and fresh.

O: the shape the mouth carves when the air is suddenly winter.

O: the moon when it is about to give birth to the thin razed version of itself.

O: is the caw of the wound alone in a cave, surrounded by vermin and bones.

O: two mouths keening.

the eye of a fish against glass
the flesh-pink fingernail of an infant
the womb-maw at crowning.

Gertrude was a false mother
Gertrude ribbed in blue, sleek
ship of war: girl-plunderer.

She will not forget it was you, O
You: the maid who made him mad
her son's stockings at his ankles
his eyes glazed and wary
his kisses pained and bloodthirsty.
He brought ghosts into his mother's bed.

She watched while
they stole your shoes
Your voice hung on metal pins
dangling tunes of cock and maidens and rue
half-rasped, *hey nonny-nonny*

she rang the bell
she locked her eyes

the door was open.

the sky bent close
the wind was right
the grass was wet
the bird said
the moon had gone.

She failed to pull loudly at your dress
She should have pulled loudly at your dress
Louder than the willow,
Come down, come home, dinner is on the table!
The bed turned, bath full and hot!
Climb into my lap, my dear child,
abhor the willow, the winding sheet of long purples!

Gertrude, ribbed in blue
watched from the hedgerow
set the hounds
at your heels
the troll under
the bridge.

Ten miles ago she could have sworn there were footprints in the sky:

Someone was tracing her path but outside and upside her.

Imprints in vapor is that possible?

The pace was her pace, the traces following her traces.

Holes sunk into the sharp waterlines.

Holes have names.

Dead men's fingers wound on her head.

Dead men's fingers pocketing the cloud. She can rip them from the ground and strangle them around her head, her hair.

There is no skin on her thigh. There is a hole where the skin should have been.

Pray you love, remember.

O

       there
you—

are (not).

dirty hem caught on a nail,
the skirting board

snags a stain

dried leaf

slap of water, of skin

(he held your wrist hard).

reddened, emboldened

it's without thinking you turn corners, turn
heads
       suspension is only fun
       for a moment

dry wet dry
fish scale the dress it was hanging you were hanging by a
thread, as they say.

said.

On the moist bank, clutch of chickweed:
how then, to fall?

All you desire is down.
All you fear, netted black feathers
Spindle beaks carve at the careful sky
onyx, measured, quiet.
Fly here soughs the water.

Dipping your eyes, they catch clouds
below the moss where the birds
cannot reach
carrion hunters
requiem in their throats
talons flicker, once:
requiem. Or concerto:
for girl, a stream,
and feathers.

It was a long walk and tangled

                    who knows
                              what you left

on branches,

        your tongue   pasted: the leaves

                    tasted you, yes,
        licked you

strand of your hair trapped on a rowan twig

did the owl see?
it was daytime, of course not.
but from behind bark?
did she sense, deep in feathered sleep,
the shiver of grief:
sharp, fennel;
pungent, rosemary;
dank, rue.

her hair is wet.
She sings in no tune:
o how the wheel becomes it the wheel becomes it the wheel becomes—
which (she wonders) is more real:
the girl in the water, or
the sky in the water?
the girl in the water, or
the sky in the water?
the girl in the water, or
the sky in the water?

She said:

> *I think nothing, my lord.*

How could she do that? Where was her fight?
When he held her wrist hard and pushed her down?
I think nothing.
O to drown that nothing!

To see and not un-see.
Scars, light:
how the wound caws
before it sinks
finding shape
somewhat like a bird's neb
sharp, for plucking
seeds, lies, eyes.

Here you are not
clothed you are not
clothed you are not
you
clutching your hair
(he clutches your hair)
the blood, nameless
thick salt in your throat
sudden cut of metal
Mother! Mother! Mother!
three times (note well)
the cock crows

O

                          O

              O

O   you rat, you

rat who stole
my daughter.

Eat my sword in your unholy mouth, Rat.
Ulcer, canker.

O: I am your mother, and you are not forgot.

O is a daughter. O has a daughter. O is a mother without
a daughter. O had a daughter. O was a daughter and lost her
mother. O saw a mother who lost her daughter. O's mother
dreamt she lost a daughter. O dreamt a lost daughter. O was
lost and her mother dreamed. O not lost but unfollowed.
O was not watched. O's mother closed her eyes when they
should have been opened. O's mother had no eyes. O's mother
did not deserve eyes. O's mother had a daughter whose eyes
were stolen. O needs eyes. O needs eyes but the birds stole
them. O fell in a river. O's mother had her eyes closed. O was
watched by birds. O fell into the water. O's mother pushed her
into the water. O's mother only thinks she pushed her into
the water. O's mother hid behind. O followed her daughter.
O walked alone. O was not alone. O's mother wanted her. O
followed the daughter to find the mother. O was the daugh-
ter. O watched the mother lose her daughter. O's mother was
a daughter. O was a mother who had no daughter. O waits.
O waits in a womb. O wants a womb to wait in. O wants her
daughter. O had a mother.
O's mother is trying to find her:
have you seen a girl dressed in dead men's fingers?

3

Little o

At 2:15 pm you climbed into the water. you fell into the water. 2:15 sky sleek with grey cloud, noon gone. the park across the road. a woman walks her dog. a man in a Wall Street suit. recess cancelled. too cold. snow coming the National Weather Service has issued a winter storm watch for two New Jersey counties in advance of a storm system that could dump as much as 6 to 7 inches of snow along with a thin layer of ice. bundled figure hunched in the bandstand lights a cigarette, to keep warm maybe. sign nearby reads: no smoking in the park. everyone smokes in this park. the only green space and basketball court for five schools and everyone else cramped into apartment blocks. the woman wears red, the dog snaps at a dead burger. they turn at the bus shelter, by the cracked swings. opposite the park is a school. opposite the park is a hospital. opposite the hospital a funeral home. a zebra crossing between them. white black white. the school made of dark brick, once an orphanage now ghost faces trapped children peer from high windows. 2:15 pm math you draw numbers on the glass in breath. through the finger marks the bodega, the library. the park. the dog. you like dogs. one day your mother promised you shall have one. 2:15 pm. you leave for the bathroom. take the pass from the hook, don't look behind you. at 2:15 pm should have looked behind you. at 2:15 you passed the boys' bathroom no you climbed a tree and then fell into the water. he held your wrist hard the door slammed. you climbed a tree and fell into the water. you fell in when someone grabbed you. no one grabbed you. he never even talked to you he told the detective. you fell by yourself. you sat with him in class and let him throw you the ball in the park. you fell because you wanted to. the water was cold. too cold. recess was cancelled. snow was coming. inches of snow along with a thin layer of ice. the man had his magazine. the woman her dog. the cold one a cigarette. 2:15 you let go of the tree. the bathroom door slammed. 2:15 he locked the stall. the tree let you go. 2:15 pm your dress snagged on a branch and the tree let you go the tree pushed you he grabbed you snagged you fell you. the sky sleek with grey. noon gone. the dog barks. quiet onslaught of snow.

It was 2:15 pm.

2:15, or thereabouts. But you can't say thereabouts. When they
question you in the room with the mirrors that you can't see
them but they can see you then you cannot say: *thereabouts.*
You have to choose a time.

2:15.

Because if you get the time wrong. If you did not check your
watch when he lured you in all you did was lean across the
door was slammed shut to the boys' bathroom locked the stall
and you were suddenly on the floor and—

if you can't remember.

only that your throat tasted of blood and salt and something
that choked and the orthodontist barked at you because
Medicaid won't pay if you wreck your own braces.

you weren't wearing a watch.

you were wearing your shorts around your ankles and your
socks were like little wads of toilet paper on the tiles. You are
flattened and blood blends with fur.

he used toilet paper to wipe the blood and wipe the cum off
your mouth.

but you didn't know that's what it was.

Did he penetrate you?

you haven't heard that word.

you hurt down there. you say. it stung. why. you threw
up. into this bag, this plastic bag they said at the
nurse's office because that's where you went even
though he made you promise not to tell. told you he
loved you. he said.

you did it. he scrawled it on a post-it note and shoved it
in your locker. his best friend cried and took the day off
school. he went home.
they didn't believe you.

you saw the principal's red bow tie float to the floor
and your arm stung and the smell of alcohol now
makes you throw up even now even
now,

they don't believe you.

The investigations, the system, the forensic interviews.

The conclusion:

She made it up. She is an intelligent, creative girl, and
apparently, that is what such girls do. And the boy stated
categorically—before he was advised to be silent—that he
had never talked to her.
It was in the police report.

The three-sentence police report, that they forgot to send the
family.

I cannot sleep, thinking
of my little o. of how she
was, before.

I cannot sleep because that day will not end.

I cannot write.
Clichés, word drugs, keep you
pretending that you're really
turning it all into something—
meaningful. making it all
Worth. While.

Fuck.

I take drugs, kind ones,
ones that tie me with little gold hooks to the trees.
the trees have roots, I borrow them.

when the policeman left. when the social workers shut the door. when the nurse threw out her latex gloves. when the voicemails to the prosecutor were not returned.

when it was not enough to lock the door, sleep in three layers of clothes, touch a knife to your chest, curtain your face with unwashed hair.

draw him, draw him, draw him.

when they call you a liar, when the one who harmed is free.

draw him, draw him, draw him.

when the policeman left. when the social workers shut the door. when the nurse threw out her latex gloves.

there are not enough books to hold what is drawn,
when all the words
have gone.

my little o, come here where the moss and mushrooms grow.
I will pretend I can rock us to sleep.

I gave my love a cherry that had no stone
I gave my love a chicken that had no bone
I gave my love a ring that had no end
I gave my love a baby with no crying

I need ammunition.
Words soft like
rabbits:
big eyes, no necks
clutching the grass
in the evening
what use are they
none none none. Hey
non nonny, nonny

When he raped my daughter he took
us both.
I intend to get us back.

What He Said:
(from a secretly recorded phone call)

I have so many files of these children,
these women on my desk, it's just
not worth it.

The Prosecutor's job is to do justice.

For someone to believe that this happened you have to be able
to explain away *everything*.

I understand, I have two girls myself.

There is a difference between a child having actual memories
and memories that didn't happen.

All kids have nightmares.

I don't believe that anything happened at all.

She's smart, mature. She probably read something somewhere.

Your daughter's statement suggested she liked him.

Now listen, an investigation was done.

I got into the University of Chicago and Notre Dame,
I'm a smart person.

He had a right to an attorney, and if he decides to say nothing,
that is his right.

You'll find few sex crimes prosecutors with more
experience than I have.

There's nothing more we can do if we ask and he says
he didn't do it.

Her video statement looked artistic, like something you'd see on
the Discovery Channel.

There is no medical evidence. If she had told someone at the time...

Your child had gone into the restroom with someone
of the opposite gender —

and that is

consent.

Most days, I am
raccoon fur in drifts
at the garden gate.

The investigation is closed, said the police.
I'm a smart person, said the prosecutor.
I don't have time, said the big white gruff voice that wore
a gun at his hip and a pen in his chest.

So I argued with the prosecutor. That is what mothers do.

But what about the nightmares?

All children have nightmares, he said.

Do you have a recipe for this, then? I enquired
most politely, the anger prickling
ants hot under the skin I will not stoop
so low as to make my voice like him
this big gruff white angry voice do not
tempt him to loosen the gun at his hip
to put his hand
down there.

I ask so nicely, so like a nice young mother, so
nice, so please sir so if it's no bother so if I can
spare two minutes of your time your busy
busy so many important matters to attend to reports to make files
to find guns to polish nice rich white boys to streets
to patrol skins to find
phone calls to make—

Do you have a recipe for this?

how to stop her charging across a busy road
when she sees a boy?
how to stop her avoiding children?
how not to dream, awake?
how to not hear voices?
how to not hold knives at her chest?
how to not throw off the covers and run through the house
and play the piano all loud and crashjangle when the smaller ones
sleep and the moon is up and *I can't remember*
and how not to sit up and sing over and over
with eyes closed and voice the dusty chant of dream:

when he raped me
when he put his—
here—
then—

over, over, over, over.

He is a busy, busy man.
There is a lot of work
for gruff white men with guns to do.

All children have nightmares, he
said.

In my worst times, it is me.
I sent her to that school
I was working that afternoon, until late;
midnight I got home from Manhattan
someone was killed by a bus at the Port Authority
everything was in turmoil
or was that another time?
I wasn't there for her to tell
to see her silence
to know she felt sick
went to bed at 4 pm
no dinner;
I didn't even think to ask
did she have dinner.
I saw the acne break out overnight
the hiding in the shower
going to bed fully dressed, overcoat
and jeans and sneakers
ready
she ate and ate
covered herself with fat.

In my bad times
it is me.
I should have seen it.

Later, after she told me
she became so thin, in two weeks
that she couldn't walk further
than the end of the street;
couldn't listen to music

more than two people talking
made her faint
she slept for hours and hours
all day sometimes
I couldn't touch her
without talking it through first
but not my shoulder
not my neck
never my arms
can I kiss you on the forehead
sometimes, *yes*
When all I wanted to do was wrap her up
shrink her down
find a way
any way
to stuff her back into my womb
and to never, ever
give birth to her
It's a madness
of sorts
I go back into labor
and stop it
hold the contractions
refuse to open
barricade my cervix
don't let her out—
but to keep her safe
like that
is to kill her.

But sometimes,
I think that way.
Deep down

where the goblins grow
they tell me
what I already know:
it is you
you bad
bad mother.

this is—
what is left,

after.

God be at your table.
In your sky.

poor little o.
three dried leaves
on a branch.

Lord, we know what we are,
but know not
what we may be.

a cold wind,
an empty mouth

a branch. sky. God's table.

4

A Fable:
Part II

Her mother lays shrews at the girl's taloned feet. The child ties them in bundles with her hair and saves them; she will be hungry later when the sun rises. The owl skims her belly over her daughter's hair, leads them through pines to the sand's edge. The moon wears mist. The child: she tucks stones under her tongue, for luck.

The child had no say in it, her hem hid a love untimely feathered. She kneaded bread and scraped patterns into the wet sand with her talons. *we know not what we may be,* sang the child, leaving scars on the shore. *who who who are you, when the moon is a mouth, a spoon against the grain the tenderness of pine when the bread is rising.* Her song is not a tree is a scathing scythe sweeping the wheat, dividing the grain against itself.

The villagers had none of it, the boy spied the girl tattled, the old women shook their heads and beat their carpets in the bright hot sun. The baker left his door unlocked so the stories crept in, fermented, crawled out and into the villagers' noses: no good will come of this no good at all, a bird may love a fish but where would they sleep? The villagers threw salt and planned ill in their hearts.

The baker was afraid, so they were stealthy, the feathered ones. In the forest evenings the girl tangled her talons in moss and roots, seeking out the still places where her mother might sing to her. The girl's mother swooped from branches, caressed her daughter's hair with mouse-breath and vertebrae of vole and squirrel. She could no longer follow her into the house or the barn or the kitchen where the bread rose, and the fire burned in the oven.

Stories cooked up by fear can be heavy; like sorrow they have a way of causing the heart to sour. The baker fought them with forgetting, and when the moon rose, locked the door. His beloved no longer visited when the salted night wind blew dank from the bay. The owl forged into the hollows and less and less the man came for her, until his smell was poetry barely remembered and mushrooms sprouted again for it was autumn once more, and damp.

The bird he had loved watched from the skeleton tree, her eyes flickered it was quiet as a mountain like fur like hunger under the skin.

At the harvest moon her mother did not come. The girl burned her hands in the fire, pitting one pain against another. The owl hid and listened to the wind that bristled with a girl crying.

The girl child with two mouths had bound her taloned feet in brine and pine needles then dry grass salvaged from the edge of the woods because the children had found her, stripped off her shoes and taken them far away to the where the sea licked the rocks. The girl hid her feet in loaves of fresh bread. But bread grows old and crumbles, and the baker beat her because that was money they could not eat.

Children are cruel, little narrow fingers splicing through feathers picking at eyes at hair and lift up your skirt lift up your skirt the men too, what is it that they want, they want to see because they believe their eyes have hands are merchants. She went to the sea-licked rocks, plied off the black shells with their knife edges, scraped at the wretched skin on her claws. Under the moon blood looks dark like syrup molasses, her feet smell like steel.

They chased her and locked the door and on the floor they forced her to show them her feet, they wiped on them blood from her own mouth on the tiled floor they made her lie down sing from her two mouths *open your mouths and sing* and it was not singing that noise it was not singing and she stuffed toilet paper into the spaces it was wet she was wet the mouths leaked on her clothes.

All the while her mother was behind bark, wrapped in silence.

The girl could not walk home so dug herself into the sand, waited for the tide to claim her. Feathers brushed her shoulder and her own trembled in reply then a shadow yes even at night there are shadows, but this one had breath and warmth. The girl slept. All night the baker searched and when he found his child he gathered her up like fallen fruit, kicked over the blood traces with sand. He carried her over the flagstone threshold. That day there was no bread.

She was a baker's daughter with long brown hair, taloned feet and wide eyes like an owl and now she locks herself inside the great ripping the tearing the siphoning of words out of her mouths and this is what she grieves: the finding of words, how they run down your cheeks the way words climb deep in the oven of your belly. they smell like bread rising.

It was time to find her mother: a long walk it was for a girl with
two mouths and taloned feet. The village road was cobble then
earth then blackberry tangling with hemlock the red roots,
fungi twisting on weathered bark oak elm rowan pine muffling
the ocean to a hoarse throat-swell.

The briars turn to stones, then sand. There is no boat. But a large piece of driftwood. The girl takes off her skirt and with it lashes herself to the wood. The water is cold and fierce, her talons curl as waves haul her, foam in her nostrils she can no longer swim. The sun trailing pale ash on the water. A cry. It is not her own. The waves change their mind tide turns shore drags her apace then feathers warm feathers about her face a beak slashing at the skirt and she is on the sand, wings cover her, feathers a blanket and the owl is singing.

The owl came to her daughter and carried her from the sand to a far cave, and the entrance was an O and inside the O was dank earth festered with bat droppings mouse shines crushed into tiny specks like flour. The girl shivered and did not look up, felt with her skin on the dark dust.

The girl had no voice because her throat was plundered with terrible grief. Her mother wept over the feathers and sang her throat into hollowness. The silence roared from the girl's guts into the cave, and the owl called her name and the owl called her name.

A Sound that Rendered Silence
A Conversation with Niki Tulk & Jerrod Schwarz

There are so many aspects and angles of O to dive into, but I want to start with something foundational to the text: fables. What fables, myths, legends, or traditions informed your writing of these poems? Was this an aspect you planned out, or did it occur more organically? Perhaps more specifically: what led you to connect fable and trauma?

I think to answer that, I need to actually address the work in con-text of the multi-disciplinary project that it is a part of, as the myth-ical element—and the ways this permeated the text—arose out of what came before it. O is actually part of a triptych: three works, span-ning several different but interrelated media. The first work, *Ophelia | Leaves*, was a performance and sonic/material art installation that re-imagined Hamlet's "to be or not to be" soliloquy from Act 3, Scene 1 of *Hamlet* as a portal into the psychic landscape of Ophelia. The sec-ond part of the project has been O. The third piece in the triptych, *Cutis Ex Libra* (or *Book of Skin*), was an installation using film, audio record-ings, and objects. This last work examines violence against women through the material practice of writing and book-making, focusing on the macabre 19th century practice of binding texts in female, hu-man skin. The center of that exploration was the story of 28-year-old Irish immigrant Mary Lynch, whose skin was non-consensually used by her autopsy doctor after her death to bind books on female anato-my and reproductive systems. They were not planned as a triptych but emerged from each other—beginning from the solo show.

I was initially drawn to the idea that William Shakespeare's cre-ation of Ophelia involved a kind of textual violence. Shakespeare is a founder of western dramatic literature and culture, almost god-like now to many people; accordingly, due to his powerful cultural posi-tion, Ophelia has become an iconic figure: the wronged maiden who loses her mind and destroys herself in response to betrayal. The na-ture of that authorship grants Ophelia a representative authority that she might not otherwise have—she is not just *a girl* who dies of be-trayal and madness, but *the girl* (as defined by Shakespeare). I want-ed to contest Shakespeare's construction of Ophelia and through this unpack how "woman" is written and framed. In *Ophelia | Leaves*, I delved specifically into how female sexual trauma can be re-written and "understood," but in such a way that her complexity and lived experience is obscured. The working-through of these concepts birthed the other two parts of the project. The more detailed research into anthropodermic bibliopegy, for example, had its source in writing from Ophelia | Leaves. The poetry manuscript initially contained sections about Mary Lynch, which I then removed as it became clear that the real, and dual, center was Little o and Big O. (Mary's story then became the core of the final installation piece.)

I followed my intuition into the realm of folklore and fable: the interlacing of the magic and the real, having animals that speak and words that sometimes are loosed from their normal syntactic moorings. The wolves who appear on trails or at the edges of a forest, preying on the child who is drawn by the mystery and forbidden nature of the woods, for example, or the many tales where a human, changed into an animal or bird, is freed by intimate, unconditional connection with another human. Eventually, I chose a monologue from the solo performance and began the manuscript from there. The monologue is about a woman traveler who comes to an inn, and because it is full, sleeps the night in a tree. A bird comes to her and offers to exchange the woman's feet for its wings, and she agrees. The woman then begins a new and strange life as a bird. In "O" the woman became an owl, and then the nursery rhyme of the owl and the pussycat came to me: this image of two unlikely partners in a pea-green boat, sailing the ocean under the moon with their jar of honey. There was something so absurd, so sad and also beautiful about this image. Ophelia says out of her trauma-induced state that, "they say the owl was a baker's daughter. Lord, we know what we are, but know not what we may be." This line haunted me, and my owl then fell in love with a baker, and they had a child: a daughter with taloned feet who was bullied by the townspeople because of what lay under the hem of her dress. The tale became one of difference, rejection, of a forced separation of mother and daughter. The daughter is attacked, she flees and in her deep pain tries to drown herself. She is saved by the owl mother, who takes her to a cave and speaks the girl's name, helping her find who they both are again.

The year before this project, an event occurred in my own family that brought back earlier traumatic experiences from my own childhood. Two different state-led investigations later, I was exhausted. I had PTSD without realizing it and no time or resources to treat the PTSD, even had I known that's what was plaguing me. After I had finished creating the solo show, it was clear the material had not finished with me yet. I wrote a lot of the Big O section, thinking there was just so much more about Ophelia to discover. Then the "unsymbolized phantom" emerged and I needed to dive in. I had to write what had happened. Writing is not therapy (for me). It does not heal—it intrudes. It insists I follow it, and then I have to find words for all this unnamable stuff that rises in my synesthetic brain. My first draft poems in the final section, what became "Little o," began as angry, long, and confused. They were thick with phrases that needed to be stripped away. It was as if I had to write the coverings before I could write what was underneath them. Some of the poems include found phrases, such as those lifted from a secretly recorded phone call with a State Prosecutor. Those words don't sound real, even though they are—and this shocked me. It was terrible to see that the truth was not believable when written down. It is also unbelievable that a man would take a woman's skin, tan it in a chamber pot, keep it for eighteen years and then cover a book. The worst, the truest things, cannot be believed. I had to work to make them true. And the gaps in memory, the times of zoning out in dissociation, the times of freezing and not being present—somehow these were in the white spaces on the page. I resisted writing this most difficult part of the manuscript because I did not want pity from readers. If I wanted anything, it was probably anger. I wanted people to march, to sign petitions, to listen to women and girls' stories. I wanted people to get angry about the enculturation of boys, the way our culture grooms. But instead of anger in my work, what seemed to open up was a vast space of mourning. The river after Ophelia's body is gone. A grey dank sky over Elsinore. Over North America.

I decided that there was a fictional and real pattern, this taking of the girl and writing her, binding her, using her own skin against her. I became deeply suspicious of text, of language, even as I used it to express myself. Working with language in a written way, especially after working through these concepts in the performance, installation and design languages, was hugely challenging.

Sometimes what I wanted to write instead was pages and pages of spirals, each with a tiny owl eye in the center. I wanted to cover pages and pages with o's. But words, even though so problematic to me, are able to index, even to bridge something— perhaps somehow point to a larger, more complicated embodied experience. An archive cannot possibly cover every inch of space. It is by its nature a curation of fragments. Putting words together on a page involved spaces between the words, around them. Those spaces were full of what cannot ever be said, maybe not even adequately indexed. They became as significant as what I actually wrote.

Your confession that "the worst, the truest things, cannot be believed...I had to work to make them true" speaks so much to the strengths in this collection and of poetry in general. As poets, we are always working slightly adjacent to more objective methods of record keeping such as documentary or photography. What advice (or precautions) would you have for other poets writing about trauma and agony? What can the poem do that other forms of media cannot?

Well, to address the first question, I believe that everyone handles their wounds in their own way, so I feel wary of speaking into any other experience than my own. What I would feel comfortable to share is how helpful it is to listen deeply to your own body, to check in with yourself, to notice where you need to dive deeper and where you are not ready to go yet. I took a lot of time to spiral my way into the material, and I allowed that long space of indirect exploration. I'd let poems sit there to breathe for months sometimes before I went back to them. I thought carefully about the difference between what I needed to write, and what parts of that wanted to be performed in a more public way. Some words were just for me, and some needed to go outside of my own sphere. Knowing this difference was hard sometimes, but time and distance, and then using physical performance to sort through things really helped with that decision making. I guess I was also very aware of not retraumatizing myself or anyone else—as much as that is possible. I didn't want to add more wounds to the shared human burden, but I also know that poems can help act as a witness in a helpful way. I resonate with what poet Cecilia Vicuña says about healing intent in the work. That can sound problematic—I mean, how could we ever presume that our artistic work might heal anybody—but I think what she means is a desire to weave things together in some way that moves towards wholeness without the homogeneity, like the way she weaves the sides of roads and rivers "together" with yarn, or the complicated voices she gives rivers and oceans.

This is an agonizing and vital collection of poems that grapples directly with sexual assault and its surrounding trauma. Having discussed the mythical inspirations of *O*, I also wanted to learn more about what pieces of modern media informed your writing on such a harrowing topic.

I have done years of research into trauma literature because I had to when my own life felt like it was falling apart, and that work now informs my practice on every level. I have a book coming out this year that chronicles a lot of that research and its intersection with art-making. I wanted to know everything. I am still wanting to know everything, but now from a more clinical perspective because I think we can all help each other heal and I want to be part of that. Judith Herman's book *Trauma and Recovery* was groundbreaking when it was first published, and also for me when I read it—it is so urgent and life-giving. Bessel van der Kolk's *The Body Keeps the Score* was essential, and then I was greatly helped by research provided by the National Child Traumatic Stress Network and RAINN.org ... and this was just the beginning. I had got to know the folx at MESA in Boulder (Moving to End Sexual Assault) and working with two friends to create a show around PTSD from sexual assault, which we took to Australia, and that involved a lot of deep research and working together. I got so much from early French feminists, like Hélène Cixous and Julia Kristeva. I spend most of my days with college students, and have the sort of relationship with them where I have heard hundreds of stories. Each one breaks me apart. Gendered violence is so much a part of the social fabric—it really is everywhere.

In her passionate essay, "The Laugh of the Medusa" (1975), Hélène Cixous throws out a call to women to not only write, but write from their bodies. She urges them to write from experiences and desires that rebel against the identities designated for them by male writers and publishers—and by society as a whole. "I shall speak about women's writing: about what it will do," she declares. "Woman must write her self: must write about women and bring women to writing, from which they have been driven away as violently as from their bodies—for the same reasons, by the same law, with the same fatal goal. Woman must put herself into the text—as into the world and into history—by her own movement" (875). Questions regarding how to put myself (let alone another woman—Ophelia or Mary Lynch) into a *text by movement*, how to *write herself*: these impelled me throughout. I have drawn from Cixous' connection of movement with writing, and the way she weaves together metaphors of the woman's body as landscape. Cixous' writing feels like dispatches from that landscape, territorial maps—maps that move, breathe, that have desires. Although at times essentialist in her views on "women writers" and "women's voices"—and even "women's bodies"—there is something in the untempered passion of Cixous' essay, her battle cry for women writers to take up the challenge of discovering what language can be when it is not simply borrowed from a hegemonic and patriarchal linguistic system, that invigorated my journey writing "O." Even though it came after the solo show, I still wrote many of the poems in the studio, moving the words and silences to feel them out.

This is also a visually fascinating collection, and one of my favorite elements of your style is the use of the prose poem. This is a bit of an impossible ask, but I want to know how you personally define what a prose poem is. Perhaps more than any other form, the discourse around exactly what prose poetry is feels miasmic, and I am always interested to hear what other writers' thoughts are!

For me, it is when a specific, unnamable *something* happens, and I can't render it in words that have that sculptural quality to them—I need strings of things, threads of them. Words in threads. Because I just can't get at it precisely, so I drape these word-strings around the thing and hope that they drape it enough to get a feel for what is underneath. To be synesthetic for a moment, they feel like contained installations of thread or fabric inside a single room. I suppose it gets called a poem because it is contained in some way— the piece has tight edges, even visually—and it does not spread itself out over multiple pages. I also like that it is so hard to define what it is!

You are a multi-disciplinary artist working in theater and performance. How has that artistic practice informed your writing? Specifically, did the physicality of that art form play a part in the writing of O?

There is a wonderful performance studies scholar, Peggy Phelan, who writes that trauma cannot be linguistically expressed, that trauma is, in effect, an experience that remains unrepresentable. "The symbolic cannot carry it," she concludes. "Trauma makes a tear in the symbolic network itself" (1997: 5). But if trauma can't be represented, it feels also true that it *demands* to be represented in some way—it enacts a version of itself again and again, performing itself, as if trying to find a way into disappearance; although it never really goes away but plays into the thread and weave of who we are. As a feminist writer, theatre-maker, and performer researching through a lens of trauma theory, I find myself in a space where word, performance, and the female body are constantly intersecting: a kind of liminal state that involves both presence and dissipation. I am curious as to whether a new poetic language might be invented in order to reflect this—to both speak and not speak.

At this point it makes sense to return to "O" as part of a constellation. The locus for each piece is the life of one specific woman. In *Ophelia | Leaves*, she is Ophelia from William Shakespeare's *Hamlet*. In the poetry manuscript, Ophelia is once again the focus for the first section (called "Big O"), but she metamorphoses into the child, "Little o." In the installation, the focus is the story of Mary Lynch. Each piece investigates what role writing—as material and embodied textual practice—plays in liberating a silenced voice, but also how writing might become culpable, even a tool of violence. I explore, for example, to what extent books bind women's voices so they can be heard, and yet also bind women's voices so they are suppressed. The manuscript came out of *Ophelia | Leaves* specifically, and included whispered recordings of Ophelia's lines, ambient soundscapes, embodied narrative, and live musical performance. The audience wandered the space, touching and viewing the material elements; I performed choreographed movements to voiceovers, spoke monologues and fables, sewed books with my hair, stripped layers of clothing from my body, and planted a garden of porcelain doll arms that I plucked from the river and collected in a basket. Over the course of the play Ophelia made a garden from the ravages of her experiences, and the planting was of disembodied child's arms, writing implements, dead leaves, and shreds of paper. An expansive river of open books wound across the performance space. It consisted of self-help books, texts on female anatomy and pathology—books that ranged from an outdated DSM book (*Diagnostic and Statistical Manual of Mental Disorders*) to *Red*

Riding Hood, to the humor of *Code Switching: How to Talk so Men will
Listen*. The choice of books was melancholic as well as comedic—a
river of diagnostic writing on what is wrong with women, how they
can be fixed, how their wounds can be labelled, dealt with. This riv-
er both attempted to explain Ophelia, at the same time that it also
drowned her.

This forty-foot-long "river" of open books ended at a rotary
clothesline hung with sheets—both sheets of music and cotton bed
sheets covered with original poetry. One sheet, hanging taut and
facing the main part of the space, doubled as a projection surface for
an intermittent series of darkly humorous, youtube-styled "how
to" videos performed by another, quirky and gregarious version
of Ophelia, on topics such as how to avoid falling in love and how
to stay safe in the water. A nine-foot-long dress of raw silk hung
suspended from the lighting grid so that its length bridged the sky
and ground. It had been hand-dyed/steamed with local plants, and
functioned also as a projection surface. Throughout the work, the
textile artist/costume designer was present on-stage: she sat at a
table, rolling reams of silk crushed with leaves and winding them
around with red spools of thread. Yards of dyed red muslin tendrils
were draped across the space, eventually bleeding into a grand pi-
ano, forming a sort of web that connected the weaving woman on
one side of the space, to the piano player on the other.

A male voice was rendered in occasional voice-overs, speaking
over and somewhat into the space, but also disconnected from this
world. The female voice, in contrast, expanded and multiplied—
not only Ophelia the maiden was present, but also the lives Ophelia
would not and could not ever live. In short, the space was limin-
al, resonant with the ghosted lives of the ghost Ophelia: Ophelia
the lover, the mother, the traveler who becomes a bird, the crone,
the storyteller, the teacher. At the heart of all these representa-
tions—of the piece itself—was communicating one young wom-
an's trauma. My own body was the container for all the Ophelias in
the show, and these different versions clashed, spoke, yelled, and
sang. Sometimes I was the old woman, other times the young girl,
at others more of an essence given human form as I made a book,
washed sheets in the river of books, stripped off clothes, and of-
fered the audience fables. I wanted to explore what it was to inhab-
it a constellation of Ophelias, the splitting off of parts of the self

in order to try and make sense of the devastating nature of trauma. Books and words became vital objects and forces in their own right, as both *critique of* and *invitation to* written language: to consider in what ways writing can both bind and liberate the female voice. Both silence and sound were paramount as other "bodies" in the space, with their own materiality and voicing of themes and content; the work, in many ways, became about sound that rendered silence.

So, that was the performance part. I had explored the labyrinth of worlds that opened out from the character of Ophelia, and written as much for performance as I could; I felt I had exhausted those possibilities for the moment. Yet I still felt that there was more to write. This unsettled feeling opened the way for the poetry manuscript. I began with pulling out pieces from the original script, finding the parts that felt like they might have a new life on paper. I returned to Cixous' words: "Woman must write her self: must write about women and bring women to writing, from which they have been driven away as violently as from their bodies—for the same reasons, by the same law, with the same fatal goal. Woman must put herself into the text— as into the world and into history—by her own movement" (875). But I was still not ready to write myself—I had a feeling at the back of my mind that this was what I would need, eventually, to do, but I felt pulled to writing more about Ophelia and Mary Lynch. So I took lines from *Hamlet* and riffed off them, intertwining with the pieces of the script. As I began to write what would become the final poems, I unpacked Ophelia's walk across the moors to finding the willow, the climb, the moment before she fell, the moment of falling. Caruth, in *Unclaimed Experience: Trauma, Narrative and History*, points out the repeating ideas of "departure" "falling" "burning" or "awakening" in work that has come out of, or reflects, trauma (5) and notes that such narratives become "inextricably bound up with the problem of what it means to fall ... The story of the falling body" (7). This suggests movement and embodiment as being a central way to express and communicate trauma; performance can be a site for such motion in a way that fixed marks on a page can never be—but nevertheless I tried. I set myself the task of writing poetry imbued with, and inspired by Caruth's sense of the falling body.

The first set of poems I developed were a series titled "Big O." Following on from the ways I had cut up (autopsied?) the words in *Hamlet* in order to find ways to perform them, I pulled apart the details of the language. I looked up the herbs Ophelia distributes in the play and made lists of their medicinal uses and folk symbolism. I wondered whether any of them were actually native to Denmark— they were not, it turned out, so I sought out their regional botanical equivalents, then researched their uses and connections with the female body. I borrowed a Shakespeare lexicon and made lists of words that were important to me, noting how often or rarely they were used. There was something almost clinical in my approach to many of the poems, as if I were trying to uncover the skeleton, the mechanics of words, to find what gave them their bodies.

From here, many of the poems were written from the voice of one who watched Ophelia from a distance, feeling for her but unable to help, as if there were a thick window between. In no poem do we actually hear Ophelia's voice—she inhabits the poems both as construct and apparition. I wrote the landscape I had been trying to create in performance; the mood was the same, and now I was writing into this space that was all at once myth, psychic landscape, and real-and-imagined environment. I was influenced by Kristeva's research into linguistic practices that have more to do with myth, poetry, and art in that they are "irreducible to the language object" (22). And yet as I wrote, I was, paradoxically, also searching for that language object. I was, in fact, trying to do both: to index a place and grief I could not describe, with words and concrete objects, forms—with language objects, of sorts. I was attempting to contain both the knowable with the unknowable. I was seeking to repurpose my own language in order to try and make something new—something that might allow what is behind (or underneath) the language to peek through. I placed, sometimes scattered, the letter "o" through-out, wondering if this letter, that was also a hole or portal, might work as an actual language object. A little mouth that might speak. That could not speak. There was something about it that was complete (a circle) and incomplete (the beginning of a word). I inserted o's amidst the poems, to fragment them and interrupt their flow, as well as open up little round conceptual doorways that could invoke some of the imaginary tunnels I had gone down in my research.

The Phelan quote reminds me a lot of *Tsunami from Solaris*, an essay collection from Aase Berg. In the eponymous essay, Berg asks,

"Why is similarity scarier than authenticity? Why is the copy more dangerous than the original? Why is the poem such an insult to the cruelty of life itself?" These questions are predicated on some big assumptions, but the emotional appeal is clear and wrenching: how can we truly connect text to trauma? You optimistically hope for a "new" language of poetics that might better bridge this gap. What does this language look like? More specifically, what does the environment around poetics look like for this language to blossom?

These questions are exactly the ones that drive my book coming out with *Routledge* this year, *Performing the Wound: Practicing a Feminist Theatre of Becoming,* and even with a book spent exploring all this, I still have no conclusions—only a constellation of "personality traits" that emerge as I explore the work of different artists. I don't think that this sort of poetic language attempts to document an event or experience exactly—in the sense of *re-presenting* it as if it were the first time happening. I think instead it takes up the idea of existing in the slippage between the copy and the original, maybe a bit like Homi Bhabha's Third Space, that space between two cultures that contains both the oppression and the response, and in that site that is liminal, the pain of the trauma might be repurposed or experienced differently—maybe the pain might be transformed or transmuted in some way. I wonder if text in this sense becomes both more material and also fluid—not so tied into normative syntax or even usage. Maybe it becomes made of several media at once? Maybe it is subsumed in light, or sound. Perhaps it is text marked on the body. Or it *is* the body. I realize this all sounds amorphous, but it seems to be there in the struggle Paul Celan had, writing his Holocaust experience in German but needing to change that German, re-imagine it.

You have asked what an environment around poetics might look like for this language to blossom, and I wish I could answer that one! Perhaps the most important thing would be a space of no judgment—where words or gestures could emerge into an environment of curiosity, of compassionate observation. Language is so fraught, so beautiful and capable of materiality, texture and energetic charge that can be quite physical. So maybe giving words an environment in which they might move amongst other media, so that they don't have to do all the work. A word could be breathed, painted, made through clay, projected, created out of mud, and then washed away. And time, of course—the language needs time to gather itself, at least in my experience. If there are others to help hold that space, to share in some way with the making or supporting that making—I have always loved when I can have at least one being (could be four-legged) to be present, amplifying that non-judgement and care. Lots of wonderful things other than poetics could blossom in such a space—it's a dream place!

In terms of how we can connect text to trauma, maybe text is a series of markers on a large space of white (mourning, grief, death in some cultural contexts), a set of unfinished trails whose smallness means that we see all that silence around them. Without those markers, the silence might blanket us so that we don't even perceive it—it might become invisible, and then we would miss the whole energetic charge around those words. Text is also scary, though, because it risks betraying what happened by that very fact of its inability to represent that white space. We need the truth of our experience, of how we experienced it, to be witnessed; there is this drive to make it complete in that way, to remember. We need others to hear what we remember and say back to us, "yes, this is what happened. This is it exactly." So words are a way we do this, but again it's like only having a few rungs on a ladder—we can't render accurately what happened because our brains experience trauma in that place that is as far from the context-making, languaging frontal cortex as it is possible to get. Where the trauma takes place is in the part of our brains that has no language. Text-making, then, is an act of translation, but from a language that had no words to translate *from*. Perhaps this is why poetry is so bewildering to work with, so necessary and yet so incomplete. It is agonizing. Words act like threads that can weave us to something, so we are joined in some way even though we are still separate. Maybe they keep us in our own subjectivity container for our protection? Acting less as bridges, and more like solitary birds that fly from one side of the river to another, dropping seeds of what is in that other land.

Photography by Maundy Mitchell

Niki Tulk is an ex-pat Australian, and experimental theatre-maker, improviser, writer, poet, and author of *Performing the Wound: Practicing a Feminist Theatre of Becoming* (*Routledge*, 2022). She lives with her family and rescue dog in the White Mountains, New Hampshire. For more details, visit her website (www.nikitulk.com).

To Jerrod and James at *Driftwood Press*, for making sure little o got the word out. Thank you for your belief in this work, your graciousness and allyship. To Julie Carr, for making sure I went as deep as I needed to and being there every step of the way. Misha Cahnmann-Taylor, Jo-Beth Allen and Michelle Bonczek told me I was a poet when I didn't believe it, and it changed everything— thank you. Tara Walker, kindred spirit poet during endless lockdown! Judith Herman, for writing *Trauma and Recovery*. Mark, best friend and fellow traveler of the abyss—we made it, scars and all. To the most beautiful dogs in the world, Charlotte and Lilly, for healing what I thought could not be healed. And to my strong, enduring, powerful daughters—you are the reasons why this world is worth walking through.

MORE TITLES FROM
DRIFTWOOD
PRESS

comics, chapbooks, & collections

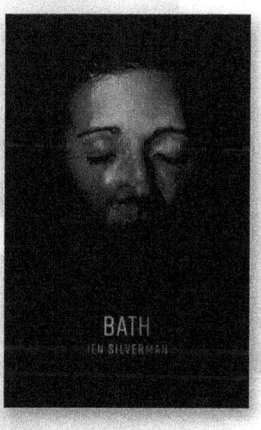

CPSIA information can be obtained
at www.ICGtesting.com
Printed in the USA
LVHW102018070722
722788LV00003B/94